AI Revolution

Artificial Intelligence

-Handbook 2023-

By Sergiu Bursuc
STUDIO538

Contents

In this handbook we will analyze how artificial inteligence can help, assist and impact some of the industries and bussiness. It will provide an overview of the potential benefits of AI and how it can be applied in different contexts.

For a more comprehensive analysis, please refer to AI Revolution.

The handbook is a useful starting point for those looking to understand the potential impact of AI on different industries and businesses and it will only provide a high-level overview of AI's potential applications and benefits, whereas the book will provide a more detailed analysis. The book will show a more detailed and comprehensive analysis and goes into greater depth on the technical aspects of AI and provides more specific examples of how AI is being used in various industries with direct links to the specific AI Software.

Benefits of using AI in your day to day activities and business

1. Personalization: AI algorithms can learn about a user's preferences and habits to provide personalized recommendations and experiences.
2. Time-saving: AI-powered tools can automate routine tasks, saving time and increasing efficiency.
3. Improved energy efficiency: AI can analyze energy consumption patterns and suggest ways to reduce energy usage and costs.
4. Faster decision-making: AI can analyze data in real-time and provide insights to support faster and better decision-making.
5. Smart homes: AI can control smart devices in a home, from lighting to heating and security systems.

6. Virtual assistants: AI-powered virtual assistants like Siri and Alexa can answer questions, play music, and even order groceries.
7. Healthcare: AI can assist doctors in diagnosing diseases and suggest treatment plans, leading to more accurate and efficient healthcare.
8. Traffic optimization: AI algorithms can analyze traffic patterns and suggest the best routes to avoid congestion.
9. Predictive maintenance: AI can monitor machines and predict when they will need maintenance, reducing downtime and maintenance costs.
10. Social media: AI algorithms can analyze social media data to identify trends and improve marketing strategies.
11. Customer service: AI-powered chatbots can provide 24/7 customer support and handle simple queries.
12. Cost reduction: AI-powered automation can reduce labor costs and increase efficiency, leading to cost savings.
13. Improved decision making: AI can analyze large amounts of data to provide insights and support better decision making.
14. Increased productivity: AI can automate routine tasks, freeing up employees to focus on higher value work.
15. Enhanced customer experience: AI-powered personalization can improve the customer experience and increase customer loyalty.
16. Improved fraud detection: AI-powered systems can detect fraudulent activity in real-time, preventing financial losses.
17. Predictive analytics: AI algorithms can predict consumer behavior and help companies tailor their marketing strategies.

18. Quality control: AI-powered systems can monitor production lines and identify defects, improving product quality.
19. Risk management: AI can analyze data to identify potential risks and provide recommendations to mitigate them.
20. Improved accuracy: AI algorithms can process large amounts of data and identify patterns with a higher level of accuracy than humans.
21. Supply chain optimization: AI can optimize supply chains by predicting demand, improving inventory management, and reducing costs.
22. Improved hiring: AI can analyze resumes and identify the best candidates for a job, reducing time-to-hire and improving the quality of hires.

Introduction

What is artificial intelligence

Artificial Intelligence, or AI, is a technology that allows machines to think and learn like humans. It involves creating computer programs and algorithms that can perform tasks that would normally require human intelligence, such as recognizing speech, understanding natural language, recognizing images, and making decisions.

Think of it like a computer brain that can learn and make decisions on its own, without being explicitly programmed to do so. It can be used to automate repetitive tasks and improve efficiency, and it can also be used to create new products and services. For example, self-driving cars use AI to navigate the roads, and digital personal assistants like Apple's Siri or Amazon's Alexa use AI to understand and respond to voice commands.

Big corporations are using AI in a variety of ways to improve their business operations and gain a competitive edge. From Amazon, Ocado, Alibaba to banks, online shops and social media. Here are some examples:

- Customer service: Companies are using AI-powered chatbots and virtual assistants to handle customer queries and complaints. These tools can analyze customer data and provide personalized recommendations, making the customer experience more efficient and satisfactory.
- Marketing and advertising: AI can help companies analyze large amounts of customer data to develop targeted advertising campaigns. By understanding customer preferences and behavior patterns, companies can create more effective marketing strategies.
- Predictive analytics: Many corporations are using AI to analyze large amounts of data to make more informed decisions. For example, predictive analytics can be used to forecast future demand for products and services, optimize supply chain operations, and improve financial planning.
- Cybersecurity: Companies are using AI to detect and prevent cyber threats. AI algorithms can analyze network traffic patterns, detect unusual behavior, and flag potential security breaches before they occur.
- Manufacturing: AI is being used in manufacturing to optimize production processes, reduce waste, and improve product quality. For example, AI-powered robots can perform repetitive tasks more efficiently and accurately than human workers.

- Inventory management: AI can be used to manage and track inventory levels, reorder supplies when necessary, and ensure that the right products are in the right place at the right time.
- Robotic automation: AI-powered robots can be used to perform tasks such as picking and packing, loading and unloading, and moving goods around the warehouse. This can improve efficiency and reduce the need for human labor.
- Predictive maintenance: AI can be used to monitor equipment and identify potential problems before they occur. This can help to prevent downtime and reduce maintenance costs.
- Route optimization: AI can be used to optimize the routes that warehouse workers and vehicles take when moving products around the warehouse. This can reduce travel time and improve productivity.
- Demand forecasting: AI can be used to forecast demand for products, which can help to optimize inventory levels and reduce waste.
- Personalized recommendations based on user data and behavior patterns
- AI-powered chatbots to handle customer queries and complaints
- Image recognition to make it easier for users to search for products and content
- Sentiment analysis to understand user sentiment and improve products and services
- Targeted advertising based on user data analysis
- Fraud detection to protect users from scams and fraudulent behavior.

Advancements in AI technology and the increasing availability of AI tools and resources mean that AI is becoming more accessible to everyone, not just big corporations. This means that individuals, small businesses, and larger companies alike can take advantage of AI to improve their operations and gain a competitive edge.

For everyday tasks, AI-powered personal assistants and voice assistants such as Siri and Alexa are readily available to consumers. These tools can help with tasks such as scheduling appointments, setting reminders, and finding information.

Small companies can use AI to automate routine tasks such as data entry, customer service, and accounting, freeing up time and resources to focus on growth and development. For example, AI-powered chatbots can handle customer queries and complaints, while predictive analytics can help small businesses forecast demand and optimize inventory levels.

Large companies can also benefit from AI in a variety of ways, including predictive analytics, fraud detection, and supply chain optimization. With the increasing availability of AI tools and resources, even smaller departments within large organizations can now take advantage of AI to improve their operations and decision-making.

Overall, the increasing accessibility of AI means that individuals, small businesses, and larger companies can all take advantage of AI to improve efficiency, increase productivity, and drive innovation.

Introduction to ChatGPT

To talk about ChatGPT we going to start with founding company and one of the big players in AI: OpenAI.

OpenAI is an artificial intelligence research laboratory consisting of the for-profit corporation OpenAI LP and its parent company, the non-profit OpenAI Inc. It was founded in 2015 by a group of high-profile tech leaders and investors including Elon Musk, Sam Altman, Greg Brockman, Ilya Sutskever, and Wojciech Zaremba. The company is headquartered in San Francisco, California.

OpenAI's mission is to advance artificial intelligence in a way that is safe and beneficial for humanity. To achieve this goal, the company conducts research in areas such as machine learning, robotics, and artificial general intelligence, and also works to promote responsible AI development and deployment through initiatives such as its AI principles.

It uses GPT-3 (short for "Generative Pre-trained Transformer 3") is a language generation model developed by OpenAI.

ChatGPT works by predicting the next word in a sequence based on the context of the previous words. It does this using a type of neural network called a transformer, which is able to process input sequences that are much longer than those typically used in other types of neural networks.

Some of the tasks that is capable of performing include:

- Language generation: GPT-3 can generate human-like text in a variety of styles and formats, including news articles, stories, and poetry.
- Language translation: GPT-3 can translate text from one language to another with high accuracy.
- Text summarization: GPT-3 can generate concise summaries of longer texts.

- Question answering: GPT-3 can answer questions based on a given context.
- Sentiment analysis: GPT-3 can analyze text to determine the sentiment it expresses (e.g., positive, negative, or neutral).
- Text classification: GPT-3 can classify text into various categories or labels.

On top of that it remembers what you said earlier in conversation and it will allow to provide follow-up correction if needed. To give a layer of control if you want its been trained to decline inappropriate requests.

Overall, GPT-3 represents a major advancement in natural language processing and has the potential to significantly impact a wide range of industries and applications.

Examples of how GPT-3 has been used in a range of applications

It has been used in a variety of applications, including language translation, summarization, content creation, and more. Here are a few examples of how GPT-3 has been used:

- Language Translation: GPT-3 has been used to build machine translation systems that can translate text from one language to another. Machine translation systems are used to translate text from one language to another automatically, without the need for a human translator. These systems can be trained to translate a wide range of languages and are used in a variety of settings, including business, government, and education. GPT-3 has proven to be particularly effective at translating languages that are closely related, such as French and Spanish.
- Summarization: GPT-3 has been used to build summarization systems that can automatically generate summaries of long texts. Summarization systems are used

to condense long texts into shorter summaries that capture the main points of the original text. These systems can be trained to summarize a wide range of texts, including news articles, research papers, and more. GPT-3 has been used to build summarization systems that can generate summaries that are accurate and easy to understand.

- Content Creation: GPT-3 has been used to generate creative writing, such as articles, stories, and poems. It has also been used to generate social media posts and marketing copy. GPT-3 has the ability to generate text that is coherent, engaging, and of high quality. This has made it a valuable tool for content creation, as it can help writers and marketers generate a large volume of high-quality content quickly and efficiently.

- Question Answering: GPT-3 has been used to build question answering systems that can provide accurate answers to user-submitted questions. Question answering systems are used to provide answers to questions that are posed by users. These systems can be trained to understand a wide range of questions and provide accurate answers in a variety of settings, including customer service, education, and more. GPT-3 has been used to build question answering systems that are able to understand and respond to a wide range of questions in a natural, human-like way.

- Chatbots: GPT-3 has been used to build chatbots that can converse with users in a natural, human-like way. Chatbots are computer programs that are designed to simulate conversation with human users. They are used in a variety of settings, including customer service, marketing, and more. GPT-3 has been used to build chatbots that are able to understand and respond to a wide range of queries and requests in a natural, human-like way. This has made GPT-3 a valuable tool for building chatbots that can provide a seamless and intuitive experience for users.

- Content generation: AI can be used to generate written content, such as product descriptions, blog posts, and social media posts.

- Copyediting: AI can be used to assist with copyediting by identifying and correcting grammar, spelling, and punctuation errors.

- Sentiment analysis: AI can be used to analyze the sentiment of written content, such as determining whether a piece of text is positive, negative, or neutral, which can be useful for determining the tone and messaging of a piece of content.

- Keyword optimization: AI can be used to identify and suggest relevant keywords that can be included in written content to optimize it for search engines.

- Content optimization: AI can be used to analyze and optimize written content, such as by identifying and removing unnecessary words, phrases or sentences, or by reordering paragraphs for better readability.

- Content summarization: AI can be used to summarize written content, such as by identifying and extracting the most important points from a piece of text, which can be useful for creating summaries of longer documents.

- Personalization: AI can be used to personalize written content, such as by tailoring the tone, language, and messaging to different audiences, or by recommending personalized content for different users based on their preferences.

- Content optimization for SEO: AI can be used to analyze and optimize written content for SEO by identifying keywords, meta-tags and other parameters that can improve the search engine ranking of the content.
- Content creation for marketing: AI can be used to create marketing materials such as emails, brochures, and flyers that are tailored to specific audiences and marketing campaigns.
- Copywriting for voice assistants: AI can be used to generate written content for voice assistants, such as Alexa or Google Home, which can be used for creating scripts for voice-enabled applications.

Introduction to DALL-E

In a few words DALL-E is a neural network developed by OpenAI that is capable of generating images from text descriptions. It is trained on a dataset of text-image pairs and can generate a wide variety of images, from photorealistic to highly stylized. DALL-E is designed to be flexible and can generate images of objects and scenes that it has not seen before.

One of the key features of DALL-E is its ability to generate images that are highly detailed and complex. It can generate images that include multiple objects and scenes, as well as images with fine-grained details and subtle variations. This makes it a powerful tool for a variety of applications, including computer graphics, design, and visual arts.

DALL-E's capabilities and how it works

DALL-E is a neural network developed by OpenAI that is capable of generating images from text descriptions. It is trained on a dataset of text-image pairs and can generate a wide variety of images, from photorealistic to highly stylized. DALL-E is designed to be flexible and can generate images of objects and scenes that it has not seen before.

One of the key features of DALL-E is its ability to generate images that are highly detailed and complex. It can generate images that include multiple objects and scenes, as well as images with fine-grained details and subtle variations. This makes it a powerful tool for a variety of applications, including computer graphics, design, and visual arts.

As an example lets say you ask DALL-E you want an expressive oil painting of a basketball player dunking, depicted as an explosion of a nebula. Although you have never seen this image or this image is not a real one, DALL-E will offer you a few options with your request.

And this is what you get:

Some examples of the types of images that DALL-E is able to generate include:

- Images of animals and plants that do not exist in the real world, such as a "dragon with butterfly wings" or a "giraffe with a crocodile's head"
- Images of objects and scenes that combine elements from different real-world contexts, such as a "desert landscape

with a spaceship" or a "modern city with medieval castles"

- Images of abstract concepts, such as "hope" or "sadness," represented through visual metaphors or symbols

Overall, DALL-E is a powerful and versatile image generation tool that is able to produce a wide range of images based on text prompts. Its capabilities are constantly evolving as the model is updated and improved by the OpenAI research team

Some potential uses for DALL-E include:

- Creative expression: DALL-E could be used by artists, designers, and other creatives to generate new and unique visual ideas.
- Advertising and marketing: DALL-E could be used to generate images for use in advertisements, social media posts, and other marketing materials.
- Education: DALL-E could be used to generate visual aids and illustrations for use in classrooms and educational materials.
- Product design: DALL-E could be used by product designers to quickly generate and test new product concepts.
- Virtual reality: DALL-E could be used to generate realistic and immersive environments for use in virtual reality applications.
- Augmented reality: DALL-E could be used to generate images for use in augmented reality applications, such as overlaying virtual objects onto the real world.
- Computer graphics: DALL-E could be used to generate realistic or stylized 3D models and environments for use in computer graphics applications such as video games, movies, and visual effects.

- Design: DALL-E could be used by designers to quickly generate and test new design concepts, such as product designs or packaging designs. It could also be used to create unique and eye-catching graphics for use in marketing materials.
- Visual arts: DALL-E could be used by artists to generate new and unique visual ideas, or to create artworks that incorporate elements that do not exist in the real world. It could also be used to create digital illustrations for use in publications or other media.

These are just a few examples of the potential applications of DALL-E. As the model continues to evolve and improve, new and innovative uses for it are likely to be developed

Introduction to Ai in image scanning

What is it and how it works

AI in image scanning refers to the use of artificial intelligence algorithms to analyze and extract information from images. It involves training machine learning models, such as convolutional neural networks (CNNs), on a dataset of labelled images to recognize patterns, objects, or features within the images.

There are several different types of AI models used in image scanning, such as:

- Image classification: It is used to classify an image into one of several predefined categories.
- Object detection: It is used to detect and locate objects within an image.
- Image segmentation: It is used to segment an image into different regions and label each region with a semantic class.

- Generative models: It is used to generate new images based on the images it was trained on.

In summary, AI in image scanning is the process of training machine learning models, typically CNNs, on a dataset of labelled images, to recognize patterns, objects, or features within the images, and using them to analyse new images.

Potential use cases for AI in image scanning:

- Medical imaging: AI can be used to analyze medical images such as X-rays and MRI scans to assist in the diagnosis of diseases.
- Surveillance: AI can be used to analyze security camera footage to detect potential security threats.
- Autonomous vehicles: AI can be used to analyze images from cameras mounted on self-driving cars to understand the surrounding environment and make decisions.
- Retail: AI can be used to analyze images of products in a store to track inventory levels and assist with restocking.
- Agriculture: AI can be used to analyze images of crops to monitor plant health and predict crop yields.
- Quality control: AI can be used to analyze images of manufactured products to ensure they meet quality standards.
- Drones: AI can be used to analyze images captured by drones to survey land, inspect infrastructure, and monitor wildlife.
- Robotics: AI can be used to analyze images from robots to help them navigate and interact with their environment.
- Facial recognition: AI can be used to analyze images of faces to identify individuals and authenticate their identity.

- Augmented reality: AI can be used to analyze images from a device's camera to place virtual objects in the real world.
- Advertising: AI can be used to analyze images of products or logos in advertising to measure their effectiveness.
- Construction: AI can be used to analyze images of construction sites to monitor progress and identify potential issues.
- Social Media: AI can be used to analyze images from social media platforms to identify objects, faces and to detect sentiments.
- Crime detection: AI can be used to analyze images from security cameras to help police identify suspects and solve crimes.
- Selfie filters: AI can be used to analyze images of faces to apply virtual makeup and other effects.

Introduction to AI Text to Video

Synthetic media refers to media content that has been generated by artificial intelligence algorithms rather than being created by humans. This can include images, videos, audio, and other types of media. Synthetic media can be generated using a variety of techniques, such as image generation algorithms, natural language processing, and machine learning.

Synthetic media has a wide range of potential applications, including creative expression, advertising, education, and entertainment. It also has the potential to be used for nefarious purposes, such as creating fake images or videos for use in disinformation campaigns.

7 types of synthetic media with examples

In recent years (or rather, months), it's become clear: We're rapidly moving towards a synthetic media future.

Technologies have matured, we've seen a surge in companies in the AI space (38 billion U.S. dollars invested in AI startups in 2021), and most importantly — AI-generated content is being used every day by independent creators and Fortune 500 companies alike.

Synthetic media is becoming a part of our daily lives.

Don't believe it? Let's have a look at some examples:

1. Synthetic video

Can you think of 3 videos you watched yesterday? Of course, you can! ☺

There's no doubt that video is taking over the internet. With attention being the new currency, video is the most engaging and therefore the most effective form of communication.

Computer generated (or synthetic or AI) video content can now be created at a fraction of the cost and effort, while still looking "real."

By removing the barriers posed by previously physical processes, companies like Synthesia are making huge strides towards accessibility and democratisation of video content creation.

2. Synthetic images

If you could get any image generated by a computer, what would it be?

It sounds like magic, but Dall-E 2 makes it possible.

Dall-E 2 is an image generation system by OpenAI that uses AI to generate images based on text input.

The technology is certainly booming right now and you've probably seen some of the fun images brought to life by AI models.

How about art, you say? Well, the system is capable of generating both realistic images and art. 🎨🖼️

Here are some of the famous examples:

Examples of AI image synthesis based on descriptions in natural language.

3. Synthetic voice

Think of virtual assistants, call centres, and dubbing in foreign languages. The majority of them still use real human voices today, but it's definitely about to change.

The difference between human and synthetic voices is becoming increasingly imperceptible, and AI simulations of real people's voices are becoming more and more popular.

You know that awkward feeling of hearing your own voice recorded? Soo cringe.

With AI voice cloning, you're able to clone your own voice or create completely new voices to fit different characters. Up to you. ☺

4. AI-generated text

Don't feel like writing? Let AI do the job for you.

You've probably heard of ChatGPT, right? It is a chatbot based on GPT3, the third-generation language model created by OpenAI that uses deep learning for generation of different text-based content, such as articles, stories, legal documents, news reports, dialogues...

It works as a normal chatbot; you ask questions or give instructions, and it will generate the answers for you. It is able to produce large amounts of high-quality text, help with research, translations, and much more.. and save you plenty of time. And yes, it can also be pretty creative.

5. AI influencers

Synthetic media also blurs the lines between where the digital realm begins and ends, and AI influencers generated by machine learning algorithms are a case in point.

Take perhaps the most famous one, Lil Miquela.

She has 3 million followers on Instagram and regularly collaborates with big fashion brands (like Chanel, Samsung, Calvin Klein...).

The algorithmically generated star describes herself as a "19-year-old Robot living in LA" and represents a completely new category of digital identities.

Is she real? Hard to say.

Is she any different from real human influencers? Hardly.

6. Mixed reality

Think Snapchat filters, furniture fitting, or — if you're old enough — the 2016 Pokemon Go mania.

These are just a few examples of mixed reality that all use technology as an additional layer to the physical environment, usually through a smartphone camera or headset.

In mixed reality, physical and virtual objects are blended, and coexist and interact in real time.

The applications (and benefits!) of mixed reality are endless, as it can be used across fields such as education, entertainment, healthcare, education, and more.

7. Face swap

Ever tried swapping your face with someone else's? It's fun, right?

There are many apps out there that use AI to detect faces in photos or videos and replace them with other faces.

This is the technology that lies behind the famous (and convincing) deep fakes of Tom Cruise and other "fake" celebrity accounts.

While face swapping seems harmless at first glance, the technology can also be used for negative purposes (e.g., revenge porn, political propaganda, or bullying).

As it's getting easier to produce synthetic content, we're already surrounded by it. Deepfakes, AI avatars, synthetic video, and AI-generated text are becoming the new (internet) normal.

Introduction to Text-to-speech AI

Text-to-speech technology is a type of software that is designed to convert written text into spoken language. It allows users to input written text, either by typing it out or by uploading a document, and then generates an audio version of the text that can be played back through a speaker or headphones.

Text-to-speech software can be used for a variety of purposes, such as:

- Providing audio versions of written materials for people with visual impairments or reading disabilities
- Creating audio versions of eBooks and other written content for listening on the go
- Generating spoken versions of written documents for use in presentations or demonstrations
- Creating audio versions of websites or other online content for easier access
- Providing voice-over narration for videos or other multimedia content

Applications of text-to-speech software in various industries

- Text-to-speech (TTS) software has a wide range of applications across various industries. Here are a few examples:
- Accessibility: TTS technology is widely used to improve accessibility for people with disabilities or reading difficulties. For example, TTS software can be used to read out text on a computer screen or mobile device, providing spoken feedback for people who are visually impaired or have difficulty reading. TTS software can also be integrated into assistive technology devices, such as screen readers, that can help people with disabilities to access information and perform tasks on a computer.
- Education: TTS software is used in education to help students with reading difficulties, to improve their comprehension, and fluency. For example, students can listen to text read out loud, which can help them to better

understand the material and improve their reading skills. TTS software can also be used to create digital books and other reading materials that can be used on mobile devices and computers. This can provide students with an alternative to traditional reading methods and make it easier for them to access written material.

- Automotive industry: TTS technology is used in automotive navigation systems, providing spoken directions and feedback to drivers.
- Customer Service: TTS technology is increasingly used in customer service to provide automated phone-based customer service. This technology can also be used to respond to text or email inquiries. It can handle frequently asked questions, route calls to the appropriate department, and provide customers with the information they need without the need for human interaction.
- Entertainment: TTS technology is used in gaming, providing spoken feedback and instructions to players, and making the game more immersive. TTS technology is also used in the entertainment industry to produce audio books, news, and other spoken-word content. With the help of TTS, content can be easily created and distributed to a wide audience in various languages.
- Mobile Devices: TTS software can be integrated into mobile devices, which can be used for various purposes like reading out incoming messages, providing spoken feedback for people with visual impairments, and many more.
- Gaming: TTS technology is used in gaming, providing spoken feedback and instructions to players, and making the game more immersive.

- Business: TTS technology is widely used in customer service, providing automated phone-based customer service or responding to text or email inquiries. It can also be used in telemarketing and other business processes, like providing automated updates on flight or train schedules.
- Healthcare: TTS technology is used in healthcare for various purposes like providing spoken instructions for medical procedures and providing spoken feedback for people with visual impairments.
- Home Automation: TTS technology is used in home automation, providing spoken feedback and instructions to users.
- These are just a few examples of the many ways that TTS software can be used in various industries.

Introduction to Ai aggregators

An AI aggregator tool is a computer program that is able to gather information from many different sources, such as databases, sensors, and online websites. This information is then analysed and processed using advanced techniques like machine learning and natural language processing to make predictions and provide insights.

It can be used in various fields such as business, research, and maintenance, and it can handle a large amount of information in real-time which is especially useful when you need current information. It can also be connected to other systems like CRM and ERP, giving you a more complete view of the information, you have.

Implementations

AI aggregators are platforms or services that collect and analyze data from multiple sources using AI algorithms. Here are 10 potential use cases for AI aggregators:

- News aggregation: AI aggregators can be used to collect and analyze news articles from multiple sources, providing a more comprehensive view of current events.
- Market research: AI aggregators can be used to collect and analyze data from multiple sources, such as financial reports and social media, to provide insights into market trends and consumer behavior.
- Sentiment analysis: AI aggregators can be used to collect and analyze social media posts and reviews to understand public opinion about a product, brand, or topic.
- Supply chain management: AI aggregators can be used to collect and analyze data from multiple sources, such as shipping and inventory data, to optimize supply chain operations.
- Fraud detection: AI aggregators can be used to collect and analyze data from multiple sources, such as financial transactions and customer behavior, to detect potential fraud.
- Personalized recommendations: AI aggregators can be used to collect and analyze data from multiple sources, such as browsing history and purchase history, to provide personalized product or content recommendations.
- Predictive maintenance: AI aggregators can be used to collect and analyze data from multiple sources, such as sensor data and maintenance records, to predict potential equipment failures and schedule maintenance.
- Network security: AI aggregators can be used to collect and analyze data from multiple sources, such as network

logs and intrusion detection systems, to detect and respond to security threats.

- Customer service: AI aggregators can be used to collect and analyze data from multiple sources, such as customer interactions and feedback, to improve customer service and support.
- Smart cities: AI aggregators can be used to collect and analyze data from multiple sources, such as traffic cameras and weather data, to improve the efficiency and liveability of cities.

Introduction to Ai gaming

AI gaming software refers to the use of artificial intelligence techniques in the development and gameplay of video games. This can include a wide range of applications, such as game development, game design, and game mechanics. Some examples of AI in gaming include:

- Non-player characters (NPCs) that exhibit intelligent behavior: One of the main applications of AI in gaming is creating believable NPCs that can interact with the player in a natural way. This can include decision making, problem solving, and emotional responses, making NPCs more realistic and engaging. For example, NPCs may react differently to the player depending on the player's actions or the in-game situation.
- Game environments that are procedurally generated: Another application of AI in gaming is the use of algorithms to create game environments, such as terrain, objects, and enemies. This can save a lot of time and resources that would otherwise be spent on manual

design and also creates unique and dynamic environments that can change every time the player plays.

- Game AI that adapts to the player's skill level and play style: AI can be used to create games that adapt to the player's skill level and play style. This can include adjusting the difficulty level, providing different challenges, and tailoring the game's content to the player's preferences. This can make the game more enjoyable and engaging for the player.

- Game AI that learns from player behavior and preferences: AI can be used to learn from the player's behavior and preferences, and use that information to improve the game's performance. This can include things like predicting the player's actions, optimizing the game's performance, and providing personalized recommendations.

- Game AI that can be used to create realistic simulations of physical phenomena: AI can be used to create realistic simulations of physical phenomena such as water, fire, smoke, and weather. This can greatly enhance the realism and immersion of the game, making it more engaging and believable for the player.

AI is used to create non-player characters (NPCs) that can make decisions, learn from the player, and adapt to the player's actions.

There are several different types of AI used in gaming, such as:

- Rule-based AI: This type of AI uses a set of predefined rules to govern the behavior of NPCs. For example, an NPC might be programmed to flee from the player if the player is carrying a weapon.

- State-based AI: This type of AI uses a set of predefined states to govern the behavior of NPCs. For example, an NPC might be programmed to enter a "fleeing" state if the player is carrying a weapon.
- Behavioral AI: This type of AI uses a set of predefined behaviours to govern the behavior of NPCs. For example, an NPC might be programmed to seek out and attack the player if the player is carrying a weapon.
- Machine Learning-based AI: This type of AI uses machine learning algorithms, such as neural networks, to learn from the player's actions and adapt its behavior accordingly.

AI in gaming typically involves training machine learning models on a dataset of gameplay experiences to learn how to make decisions and take actions that are similar to those of human players. Once the model is trained, it can be used to control the behavior of NPCs in the game.

In summary, AI in gaming is the process of using AI algorithms to create more challenging, realistic, immersive and engaging gameplay experiences by creating NPCs that can make decisions, learn from the player, and adapt to the player's actions.

Introduction to AI Research

AI, or artificial intelligence, is a computer program that can think and learn like a human. In the research field, AI is used to analyze large amounts of data and extract insights that would be difficult or impossible for humans to detect.

Imagine you have a big puzzle with many pieces and you want to find out how they fit together. An AI program can help you by looking at all the pieces, figuring out what each one looks like, and then putting them together to make a big picture. In the same way, an AI program can look at large amounts of data and figure out what it means and how it is related to other data.

AI can be used in many different ways in research. For example, it can be used to analyze medical images to detect tumours or other abnormalities. It can also be used to analyze financial data to predict future market trends.

Implementations of AI in research

AI is used in research to automate the process of analyzing data and extracting insights. This can be applied to a wide range of fields, such as medicine, physics, and social science. Some examples of how AI is used in research include:

- Image and signal processing: AI can be used to analyze images and signals, such as medical images and sensor data, to extract insights that would be difficult or impossible to detect by humans. For example, AI algorithms can be used to analyze medical images, such as MRI and CT scans, to detect tumors or other abnormalities that would be difficult for human radiologists to detect. Similarly, AI can be used to analyze sensor data from machines and equipment to predict when maintenance is needed, reducing downtime and increasing efficiency.

- Predictive modelling: AI can be used to create predictive models that can be used to forecast future events or trends. This can be used in fields such as finance, weather forecasting, and epidemiology. For example, AI can be used to analyze financial data, such as stock prices, to predict future market trends. Similarly, AI can be used to analyze weather data to make more accurate predictions about future weather patterns, which can be used to improve public safety and emergency response.

- Natural language processing: AI can be used to analyze text data, such as scientific literature, social media, and news articles, to extract insights that would be difficult or impossible to detect by humans. For example, AI can be used to analyze scientific literature to identify patterns and relationships that would be difficult for human researchers to detect, such as identifying new potential drug targets. Similarly, AI can be used to analyze social media data to detect patterns that indicate public opinion or sentiment about a particular topic.

- Automating experimentation: AI can be used to automate the process of running experiments, such as in drug discovery, where AI algorithms can be used to design and optimize experiments. For example, AI can be used to analyze large amounts of data from previous experiments to identify patterns that indicate which conditions are most likely to lead to a successful outcome. This can be used to optimize the design of future experiments, reducing the number of trials needed to find a successful outcome.

- Optimization: AI can be used to optimize complex systems, such as supply chains, energy grids, and transportation networks. For example, AI can be used to optimize the scheduling of trains and buses to reduce delays and increase efficiency. Similarly, AI can be used to optimize the scheduling of production in a factory, reducing downtime and increasing efficiency.

- Genomics: AI can be used to analyze large amounts of genetic data to identify patterns and relationships that would be difficult or impossible to detect by humans. This can include identifying genetic markers that are associated with specific diseases, or identifying patterns in genetic data that can be used to improve crop breeding. For example, AI can be used to analyze genomic data to identify genetic variations that are associated with a higher risk of developing cancer, which can help doctors to identify patients who are at a higher risk of developing the disease and take preventative measures.

- Robotics: AI can be used to control and optimize the performance of robots, such as in manufacturing and space exploration. For example, AI can be used to control the movement of robots, allowing them to navigate complex environments, and to perform tasks that would be difficult or impossible for humans to perform. Additionally, AI can be used to optimize the performance of robots, such as by adjusting the movement of the robot to minimize energy consumption or to increase the speed of the robot.

- Climate modelling: AI can be used to create simulations of the Earth's climate, and analyze historical and real-time data to predict future changes in climate and weather patterns. For example, AI can be used to analyze weather data to predict future changes in temperature, precipitation, and wind patterns. This can be used to improve public safety and emergency response by providing advance warning of extreme weather events.

- Fraud detection: AI can be used to analyze financial transactions, social media activity, and other data sources to detect patterns that indicate fraudulent activity. For example, AI can be used to analyze financial transactions to detect patterns that indicate money laundering or other financial crimes. Similarly, AI can be used to analyze social media activity to detect patterns that indicate potential terrorist or criminal activity.

- Predictive maintenance: AI can be used to analyze sensor data from machines and equipment to predict when maintenance is needed and optimize the scheduling of maintenance activities. This can help to reduce downtime and increase efficiency by allowing for proactive maintenance rather than reactive maintenance. For example, AI can be used to analyze sensor data from a manufacturing machine to predict when a part is likely to fail. This information can then be used to schedule maintenance before the failure occurs, preventing unplanned downtime and increasing the overall efficiency of the manufacturing process.

Introduction to Ai translation

AI is used in the field of machine translation, which is the use of computer algorithms to translate text from one language to another. AI-powered machine translation systems use a combination of statistical methods and neural networks to analyze and understand the meaning of text in one language and generate translations in another language.

One of the main benefits of using AI in translation is that it can handle large amounts of text quickly and accurately. This can be useful for tasks such as translating large volumes of documents, websites, or subtitles, which would be time-consuming and costly to translate manually.

How this can be used in the day to day activities you might ask. Well...

AI-based machine translation is a way for computers to turn written words in one language into written words in another language. It's like having a computer helper who can speak many different languages, it can help you understand what other people are saying, even if they speak a different language than you.

Imagine you want to read a book, but it's only available in French, and you only speak English. With AI machine translation, you can use a computer program to turn the French words into English words so that you can understand what the book is saying. This can be really helpful if you're traveling to a different country and want to read the news or a menu in a restaurant, or if you have a friend who only speaks Spanish and you want to send them an email.

AI machine translation is also used by companies and organizations to help them communicate with people who speak different languages. For example, a company that sells products online might use AI machine translation to help customers who speak different languages understand the product descriptions and instructions. This can help the company reach more customers and sell more products.

AI machine translation can be used in many different ways, and it is becoming more and more common as technology improves and more people are connected to the internet. With AI machine translation, you can understand what others are saying, even if they speak a different language. It can help you travel to different countries, read books and news, and even talk to friends and family who speak different languages.

Business communication: Companies can use AI-based machine translation to communicate with customers and partners who speak different languages. This can help companies expand their market reach and improve customer service.

Social media: AI-based machine translation can be used to automatically translate posts, comments, and messages on social media platforms, making it easier for users to communicate with people who speak different languages.

E-commerce: Online retailers can use AI-based machine translation to automatically translate product descriptions and customer reviews, making it easier for customers who speak different languages to find and purchase products.

Education: AI-based machine translation can be used to translate educational content, such as textbooks, articles, and videos, making it more accessible to students who speak different languages.

Travel: AI-based machine translation can be used to translate signs, menus, and other information in airports, hotels, and other travel-related locations, making it easier for travellers who speak different languages to navigate and understand their surroundings.

Introduction to AI avatar

An AI avatar is a digital representation of a person, typically in the form of a 3D model or a 2D image, that is powered by AI technology. The AI allows the avatar to interact with users in a lifelike and human-like manner, such as by responding to voice commands, recognizing facial expressions and emotions, and carrying out tasks.

An AI avatar is a digital representation of a human or a character that is controlled by artificial intelligence algorithms. The main purpose of an AI avatar is to interact with users in a natural and human-like way, providing assistance, entertainment or companionship.

How can avatars be used

An AI avatar is a computer program that can look and talk like a real person, it can be used in many different ways to help people.

Imagine you have a smart speaker at home, instead of talking to a computer voice you can talk to an AI avatar that can look like a person. You can ask it to play music, tell you the weather, or even make a phone call for you. It can be like having a personal assistant that can help you with many things, but it's not a real person, it's just a computer program.

Another way AI avatar can be used is in customer service, imagine you are trying to buy something online and you have questions, instead of talking to a computer voice you can talk to an AI avatar that looks like a real person. They can help you find what you're looking for, answer questions, and even guide you through the buying process.

AI avatars can also be used in education, imagine you are a student and you want to learn a new language, instead of using a computer program that only talks, you can use an AI avatar that can also show you how to say words and phrases with their mouth. This can make learning a new language more fun and interactive.

In healthcare, AI avatars can be used in virtual therapy sessions, it can help patients with chronic conditions, and help with medication adherence, it can be used to provide guidance and support to patients in a non-intrusive way.

Virtual assistants: AI avatars can be used as virtual assistants, such as in smart home devices or personal digital assistants, to interact with users and carry out tasks such as playing music, setting reminders, and controlling smart home devices.

Entertainment: AI avatars can be used in games and other forms of entertainment, such as by providing interactive and personalized experiences for users.

AI avatars can be controlled by a human operator or can be fully autonomous, capable of making decisions and carrying out tasks on their own. The technology behind AI avatars is constantly evolving, making them increasingly realistic and sophisticated, and capable of understanding and responding to users in more natural and human-like ways.

In summary, AI avatars are computer programs that can look and talk like real people, they can be used to help you with many things, such as playing music, buying things online, learning a new language, and even provide healthcare support. They can make these tasks more interactive and fun.

Introduction to Ai in marketing

AI in marketing is like having a special computer helper that can make your marketing better. The computer uses special rules and algorithms to analyze information about your customers, such as what they like and what they buy. With this information, the computer can help you create special ads and messages that will be more interesting to each customer. This is called personalization.

Another way AI can help is by looking at past customer behavior and making predictions about what they might do in the future. This can help you make better decisions about which customers to target and how to reach them. This is called predictive analytics.

AI can also help you talk to your customers in a more natural way, like a real person. You can use AI to create special computer programs called chatbots that can help customers find what they need, answer questions and even make a purchase. This can make it easier and faster for customers to get help, and can also help you save time and money.

AI can also help you improve your marketing by making suggestions about how to make your ads and messages better. It can also help you optimize your website and make it more interesting to customers. This is called optimization

Here are a few examples of how AI is used in marketing:

- Personalization: Personalization refers to the use of AI to analyze customer data and behavior to create personalized experiences for each customer. This can include personalized product recommendations, content, and email campaigns. For example, if a customer has shown interest in purchasing outdoor gear, the AI can suggest outdoor gear products to them in their next visit, or send them targeted emails about outdoor gear sales. AI can analyze customer data such as browsing history, purchase history, and demographics to create personalized product recommendations. This can increase the likelihood of a purchase, as customers are more likely to buy products that are relevant to their interests. Personalized product recommendations can be implemented on e-commerce websites, social media platforms, or mobile apps.

- Predictive analytics: Predictive analytics refers to the use of AI to analyze data and make predictions about customer behavior. This can include predictions about which customers are most likely to purchase a product, respond to a campaign or churn. For example, if an AI system notices that a customer hasn't made a purchase in a while or has shown a decrease in engagement, it can predict that the customer is at risk of churning, and the company can take actions to prevent it. AI can analyze customer data such as browsing history, purchase history, and demographics to predict future purchasing behavior. This allows companies to proactively target customers and increase sales.

- Chatbots and virtual assistants: Chatbots and virtual assistants are AI-powered programs that can interact with customers in natural language. They can provide customers with information or assistance, such as answering questions about products or services, helping customers navigate a website, or providing customer service. For example, a chatbot on a company's website can assist customers in finding the right product, answer their questions and even complete a purchase without the need for human assistance. AI-powered chatbots can provide 24/7 customer service, answering frequently asked questions and providing assistance with purchases or returns. Chatbots can be integrated into e-commerce websites, social media platforms, or mobile apps.
- Optimization: Optimization refers to the use of AI to optimize various aspects of the marketing process. This can include ad targeting, website design, and email campaigns. By analyzing data, AI can make adjustments to improve performance, such as increasing the click-through rate of an ad or improving the conversion rate of a website.
- Social Media monitoring: Social media monitoring refers to the use of AI to monitor and analyze social media data. This can include identifying patterns and trends, such as which topics are most popular among customers, and can be used to improve social media marketing campaigns
- Targeted advertising: AI can analyze customer data such as browsing history, purchase history, and demographics to create targeted advertising campaigns. This can increase the effectiveness of the advertising, as customers are more likely to click on ads that are relevant to their interests. Targeted advertising can be implemented on

social media platforms, search engines, or e-commerce websites.

- Email marketing: AI can analyze customer data such as browsing history, purchase history, and demographics to create personalized email marketing campaigns. This can increase the effectiveness of the email, as customers are more likely to open and click on emails that are relevant to their interests.

- Social media marketing: AI can analyze customer data such as browsing history, purchase history, and demographics to create targeted social media campaigns. This can increase the effectiveness of the advertising, as customers are more likely to engage with social media posts that are relevant to their interests.

- Search engine optimization: AI can analyze customer data such as browsing history, purchase history, and demographics to optimize website content for search engines. This increases the visibility of the website and drives more traffic.

- Affiliate marketing: AI can analyze customer data such as browsing history, purchase history, and demographics to create personalized affiliate marketing campaigns. This increases the effectiveness of the advertising and reduces costs.

- Influencer marketing: AI can analyze customer data such as browsing history, purchase history, and demographics to identify influencers that are the most likely to drive sales. This increases the effectiveness of the advertising and reduces costs.

- Marketing automation: AI can automate repetitive tasks such as data analysis, campaign creation, and customer segmentation. This allows companies to save time and increase efficiency in their marketing efforts. Marketing automation can be implemented in various areas of marketing such as email marketing, social media marketing, and search engine optimization. With AI, marketers can automate tasks such as lead generation, lead scoring, and customer segmentation, enabling them to focus on more strategic and creative tasks. Additionally, AI can help automate the creation and management of marketing campaigns, allowing for more personalized and effective campaigns.

AI in marketing can help companies to improve the effectiveness of their marketing efforts, increase sales, and provide a better experience for their customers. However, it's important to note that AI is not a magic solution and should be used in conjunction with human experience and expertise for best results.

Introduction to Self-improvement & AI

Personal self-improvement with AI refers to the use of AI technology to help individuals improve various aspects of their lives, such as health, productivity, and personal growth.

Some examples of use cases are:

- Personalized coaching: AI-powered personal coaching systems can provide personalized guidance and feedback to help individuals improve their skills and achieve their goals. These systems can use machine learning algorithms to analyze a user's performance, strengths, and weaknesses, and provide personalized recommendations for improvement. They can also use natural language processing and dialogue systems to provide real-time feedback and guidance, and help individuals stay on track with their goals.

- Self-reflection: AI-powered journaling or self-reflection tools can help individuals gain insights into their own thoughts and behaviours, and identify areas for improvement. These tools can use natural language processing to analyze a user's journal entries, and provide insights into patterns of thinking and behavior. They can also use machine learning algorithms to identify areas for improvement and provide personalized recommendations for self-reflection.

- Mental and physical health: AI can be used to track and monitor mental and physical health, and provide personalized recommendations for improvement. These systems can use machine learning algorithms to analyze a user's physical activity, sleep patterns, mood, and other health metrics, and provide personalized recommendations for improving mental and physical health. They can also use natural language processing to analyze a user's journal entries and provide insights into patterns of thinking and behavior that may be affecting mental health.

- Learning: AI-powered educational tools can provide personalized learning experiences, adapting to the user's level of understanding and providing tailored instruction. These tools can use machine learning algorithms to analyze a user's performance, and provide personalized recommendations for study materials, practice quizzes, and other learning resources. They can also use natural language processing to provide personalized feedback on writing, and speech recognition to provide feedback on pronunciation.

- Time management: AI-powered time management tools can help individuals optimize their schedule, prioritize tasks and manage their time more efficiently. These tools can use machine learning algorithms to analyze a user's schedule, habits, and priorities, and provide personalized recommendations for task prioritization and time management. They can also use natural language processing to understand and respond to natural language commands, for example, to schedule a meeting or call.

- Language learning: AI-powered language learning apps can provide personalized instruction and practice to help individuals improve their language skills. They can use speech recognition to track the users pronunciation, natural language processing to provide feedback on grammar, and machine learning algorithms to adapt to the user's level of understanding and provide tailored instruction.

- Nutrition: AI-powered nutrition apps can provide personalized meal plans and tracking, based on an individual's dietary needs and goals. These apps can use machine learning algorithms to analyze a user's dietary habits, and provide personalized recommendations for meals, snacks, and supplements. They can also use image recognition to scan barcodes and identify the nutritional information of foods.

- Financial management: AI-powered financial management apps can provide personalized investment recommendations and budgeting advice. These apps can use machine learning algorithms to analyze a user's spending habits, income, and financial goals, and provide personalized recommendations for saving, investing, and budgeting.

- Productivity: AI-powered productivity apps can help individuals optimize their workflow, set goals, and track progress. These apps can use machine learning algorithms to analyze a user's habits and schedule, and provide personalized recommendations for task prioritization and time management.

- Public speaking: AI-powered public speaking coaches can provide real-time feedback and coaching to help individuals improve their public speaking skills. These apps can use speech recognition to track a user's speaking rate, tone, and pronunciation, and provide real-time feedback and coaching for improvement.

- Meditation: AI-powered meditation apps can provide personalized guided meditation sessions, based on an individual's needs and goals. These apps can use machine learning algorithms to analyze a user's stress levels, mood, and sleep patterns, and provide personalized recommendations for meditation practices and techniques.

- Writing: AI-powered writing apps can provide real-time feedback on grammar, style, and readability to help individuals improve their writing skills. These apps can use natural language processing to analyze a user's text, and provide real-time feedback and suggestions for improvement.

- Study: AI-powered study tools can provide personalized flashcard sets, and practice quizzes to help individuals prepare for exams. These apps can use machine learning algorithms to analyze a user's performance, and provide personalized recommendations for study materials and practice quizzes.

- Fitness: AI-powered fitness apps can provide personalized workout plans, and track progress over time. These apps can use machine learning algorithms to analyze a user's fitness level, and provide personalized recommendations for workout routines, exercises, and progress tracking.
- Sleep: AI-powered sleep apps can track sleep patterns and provide personalized recommendations for improving sleep quality. These apps can use machine learning algorithms to analyze a user's sleep patterns, and provide personalized recommendations for sleep routines, bedtime habits, and other factors that can affect sleep quality.

Introduction to Video editing with AI

AI-powered video editing refers to the use of artificial intelligence and machine learning techniques to automate the process of editing video content.

Some benefits of using AI in video editing include:

- Efficiency: AI-powered video editing can significantly speed up the editing process by automating repetitive tasks such as colour correction and audio mixing.
- Improved accuracy: AI-powered video editing can help achieve higher levels of precision, consistency, and accuracy in the final product.
- Personalization: AI-powered video editing can be used to create personalized video content based on a user's preferences and viewing history.

- Object and face detection: AI-powered video editing can be used to detect and track objects and faces in a video, allowing for more precise editing and effects.

- Content Creation: AI-powered video editing can be used to generate new video content from existing footage, such as creating a new video from a set of images, or creating a new video from a script.

- Automated organization: AI-powered video editing can help to automatically organize and sort video footage, making it easier to find specific clips and footage.

- Real-time editing: AI-powered video editing can be used to make real-time adjustments and edits to a video during live streaming or live events.

- Automatic captioning and translation: AI-powered video editing can be used to automatically generate captions and subtitles for videos, as well as translate them to different languages.

- Virtual Reality and 360-degree video: AI-powered video editing can be used to create and edit virtual reality and 360-degree video content, providing a more immersive viewing experience.

Introduction to AI Generative code

Generative code is a way for computers to create new code or programs on their own, without human input. Think of it like a recipe: a chef follows a recipe to make a dish, but a generative code is like a chef who can create new recipes on its own.

Generative code can be used in a variety of ways, here are a few examples:

- Art and Design: Generative code can be used to create unique and interesting artwork, such as digital paintings, sculptures, and animations. It can also be used in the design of buildings, bridges, and other structures, allowing architects and engineers to explore new and innovative designs.
- Music: Generative code can be used to compose music, generate new melodies and harmonies, and create unique soundscapes.
- Game development: Generative code can be used to generate new levels, characters, and other game elements, allowing for a more diverse and dynamic gaming experience.
- Natural language processing: Generative code can be used to generate new text, such as news articles, fiction, and poetry.
- Video creation: Generative code can be used to create new videos, such as movie trailers, music videos, and commercials, using existing footage and images.
- Business: Generative code can be used in business to generate new product designs, optimize manufacturing processes, and even create new business models.
- Research: Generative code can be used in research to generate new hypotheses, models, and simulations, and to explore new areas of inquiry.
- Robotics: Generative code can be used to create new robot designs, and to control the behavior of robots in different environments.
- Fashion: Generative code can be used to create new fashion designs, patterns, and garments.

- City Planning: Generative code can be used to generate new urban design plans, and to optimize the layout and infrastructure of cities.
- Photography: Generative code can be used to generate new images and to enhance existing ones, such as by adding new effects or removing unwanted objects.
- Film: Generative code can be used to create new visual effects, animations, and special effects for film and video.
- Interactive Media: Generative code can be used to create new interactive experiences, such as virtual reality and augmented reality.
- Advertising: Generative code can be used to create new advertising campaigns, and to optimize the targeting of ads to specific audiences.
- Manufacturing: Generative code can be used to optimize manufacturing processes, and to create new products and parts.
- Agriculture: Generative code can be used to optimize crop yields, and to create new plant varieties.
- Medicine: Generative code can be used to optimize drug development, and to create new medical treatments.
- Space Exploration: Generative code can be used to optimize the design of spacecraft, and to plan new space missions.

As you can see, generative code can be used in a wide variety of fields and industries, and the possibilities are constantly expanding as technology continues to advance. Some other potential areas where generative code can be used include:

- Cybersecurity: Generative code can be used to automatically generate new security protocols and to identify and respond to potential threats.

- Transportation: Generative code can be used to optimize traffic flow, and to plan new transportation systems such as self-driving cars.
- Education: Generative code can be used to create new educational resources, such as interactive textbooks and personalized learning materials.
- Energy: Generative code can be used to optimize energy production and distribution, and to create new renewable energy sources.
- Environment: Generative code can be used to optimize resource management, and to create new sustainable technologies.
- Customer Service: Generative code can be used to create new chatbot, and to optimize the interactions with customers.
- Human resources: Generative code can be used to optimize recruitment, and to create new employee training programs.
- Supply Chain: Generative code can be used to optimize logistics, and to create new supply chain strategies.
- E-commerce: Generative code can be used to optimize pricing, and to create new marketing strategies.
- Finance: Generative code can be used to optimize investment strategies, and to create new financial products.

As you can see, the potential applications for generative code are nearly endless, as it can be applied to nearly any field where automation, optimization, and creativity is needed.

Introduction to Social media AI

Can AI help with social media?

Yes, AI can be used to help with social media in a variety of ways. Here are a few examples:

- Content creation: AI can be used to generate new content, such as text, images, and videos, for social media platforms. This can help businesses and individuals create new and engaging content more efficiently.

- Content curation: AI can be used to automatically curate content from various sources and recommend it to users based on their preferences and interests. This can help users discover new and relevant content on social media platforms.

- Social listening: AI can be used to monitor social media for mentions of specific keywords, phrases, or brands, and provide insights into user sentiment and engagement. This can help businesses and organizations understand how their brand is perceived on social media.

- Chatbots: AI can be used to create chatbots that can answer questions, provide customer support, and even make sales on social media platforms.

- Sentiment analysis: AI can be used to analyze text and images on social media platforms to determine the sentiment expressed in them, such as whether a post is positive, negative, or neutral. This can help businesses and organizations understand how their products and services are perceived on social media.

- Influencer marketing: AI can be used to identify and analyze influencers on social media platforms, and to determine the most effective ways to collaborate with them.

- Optimizing ad campaigns: AI can be used to optimize ad campaigns on social media platforms, by analyzing data such as user demographics, interests, and browsing history, to identify the most effective targeting strategies.
- Content moderation: AI can be used to monitor and moderate social media platforms for inappropriate content, such as hate speech, spam, and fake news.
- Predictive analytics: AI can be used to analyze data from social media platforms and predict future trends, such as which topics or hashtags are likely to become popular. This can help businesses and organizations stay ahead of the curve and plan their social media strategies accordingly.
- Virtual assistants: AI can be used to create virtual assistants that can help users manage their social media accounts, such as scheduling posts, responding to messages and notifications, and analyzing engagement metrics.
- Virtual reality and augmented reality: AI can be used to create immersive virtual reality and augmented reality experiences on social media platforms, such as virtual tours, live streaming events, and interactive games.
- Language Translation: AI can be used to translate text and speech in social media platforms, allowing users to communicate across different languages, which can help to expand reach to a global audience.
- Personalized recommendations: AI can be used to analyze data from social media platforms and provide personalized recommendations to users, such as recommended friends, groups, and pages to follow, and recommended content to view or share.

- Automatic summarization: AI can be used to summarize large amount of text and make it more manageable for the user, this can be useful for news, articles, and long-form content.
- Anomaly detection: AI can be used to detect unusual or anomalous behavior on social media platforms, such as identifying fake accounts or bots, detecting potential cyberattacks or fraudulent activities, and identifying potentially harmful content. This can help to ensure the security and integrity of social media platforms, and protect users from malicious actors.
- Emotion detection: AI can be used to analyze text, images, and video on social media platforms to detect emotions expressed in them, such as happiness, sadness, anger, etc. This can help businesses and organizations understand how their products and services are perceived by users, as well as detect potential issues or complaints.
- Automatic image captioning: AI can be used to automatically generate captions for images and videos on social media platforms, making them more accessible to users with visual impairments.
- Social media analytics: AI can be used to analyze data from social media platforms and provide insights into user behavior, such as demographics, interests, and engagement metrics. This can help businesses and organizations understand their target audience and optimize their social media strategies.

These are just a few examples of how AI can be used to help with social media, and the possibilities are constantly expanding as technology continues to advance.

Introduction to Ai in Music Industry

AI, or artificial intelligence, is a technology that allows computers to learn and make decisions on their own. In the music industry, AI is being used in a variety of ways to help create, produce, and promote music.

One-way AI is being used in music is to help create new songs. There are programs that use AI to compose music based on certain input, such as a specific style or mood. This means that a computer can create a song that sounds similar to a certain artist or genre without human help.

Another way AI is being used in music is to help produce and mix songs. There are programs that use AI to analyze a song and make suggestions for how it could be improved, such as adjusting the levels of different instruments or vocals.

AI is also being used to help promote music. For example, there are programs that use AI to analyze data about music listeners and make recommendations for new songs and artists they might like. This can help musicians reach a wider audience and gain more fans.

Song writing: AI can be used to compose and generate new songs based on certain input such as a specific style or mood.

Music production: AI can be used to analyze and make suggestions for improving songs, such as adjusting the levels of different instruments or vocals.

Music arrangement: AI can be used to arrange and organize different elements of a song to create a cohesive final product.

Music arrangement for live performance: AI can be used to generate a live performance arrangement of a song

Music promotion: AI can be used to analyze data about music listeners and make recommendations for new songs and artists they might like, which can help musicians reach a wider audience and gain more fans.

Music discovery: AI can be used to analyze listener data and recommend new songs and artists based on their listening habits.

Music personalization: AI can be used to generate playlists and radio stations tailored to a specific listener's taste.

Music education: AI can be used to create interactive and adaptive tutorials and exercises for music learning.

Music composition for film, video games and other media: AI can be used to generate custom music tracks to enhance the overall experience.

Music analysis: AI can be used to analyze and extract meaningful insights from large datasets of music, such as audio features and lyrics, which can be used for research and other purposes.

Overall, AI is a technology that is being used in the music industry to help create, produce and promote music in more efficient and personalized ways.

Introduction to AI in finance

AI, or artificial intelligence, is being used in the finance industry to automate and improve various processes, such as risk management, investment management, and customer service.

One-way AI is being used in finance is for risk management. AI-powered systems can analyze large amounts of data and identify patterns that indicate potential risks. This can help financial institutions make more informed decisions and take proactive measures to mitigate risks.

Another way AI is being used in finance is for investment management. AI-powered systems can analyze financial data and make predictions about market trends, which can assist portfolio managers in making investment decisions.

AI is also being used in customer service. AI-powered chatbots and virtual assistants can assist customers with their financial needs, such as answering questions about their accounts, providing account information, and helping them complete transactions.

Some other use cases of AI in finance are:

- Credit scoring and fraud detection: AI models can be trained to analyze credit data, such as credit history, income, and other financial information, to determine an individual's creditworthiness. Additionally, AI can also be used to detect fraudulent activity by identifying patterns or anomalies in financial transactions.

- Automated trading and portfolio management: AI-driven algorithms can analyze market data and make trades on behalf of investors, or assist human traders in decision making. Additionally, AI can also be used to optimize investment portfolios based on an individual's risk tolerance and financial goals.

- Risk management and compliance: AI can help financial institutions identify and mitigate potential risks, such as market fluctuations or regulatory compliance issues. It can also monitor and report on financial activities to ensure compliance with laws and regulations.

- Predictive maintenance for financial infrastructure: AI-powered predictive maintenance can help financial institutions anticipate and prevent potential infrastructure failures, such as system outages or network disruptions.

- Customer service and virtual assistants for financial institutions: AI-powered virtual assistants can provide customers with quick and accurate responses to their questions and help them resolve issues, without the need for human customer service representatives.

- Fraud detection in insurance claims: AI can be used to analyze insurance claims and detect patterns or anomalies that may indicate fraudulent activity.
- Predictive modelling for financial forecasting: AI can be used to create predictive models that analyze historical financial data to forecast future market trends and inform investment decisions.
- Targeted marketing and customer segmentation: AI can be used to analyze customer data and identify patterns, allowing financial institutions to target marketing efforts and tailor products to specific customer segments.
- Chatbots for financial advice and investment recommendations: AI-powered chatbots can provide financial advice and make investment recommendations to individuals based on their financial goals and risk tolerance.
- Blockchain-based smart contracts for financial transactions: AI can be used to automate financial transactions using blockchain-based smart contracts, which can reduce the need for intermediaries and increase the efficiency and security of financial transactions.
- Algorithmic trading: AI can be used to develop algorithms that can automatically make trading decisions, such as buying or selling stocks, to take advantage of market conditions.
- Portfolio management: AI can be used to analyze financial data and create diversified portfolios, which can minimize risk and maximize returns, helping financial institutions

and individual investors to make more profitable investments.

- Investment management: AI can be used to analyze financial data and identify investment opportunities, such as stocks or bonds, helping financial institutions and individual investors to make more profitable investments.

Introduction to AI Image improvement

Image enhancement is the process of improving the visual quality of an image. It can be used to correct for various types of image degradation such as blur, noise, and low contrast.

There are several ways that AI can be used to enhance images, including:

- De-noising: AI models can be trained to remove noise from images, by identifying and removing pixels that are not part of the true image.
- Sharpening: AI models can be trained to sharpen images, by enhancing edges and fine details.
- Contrast enhancement: AI models can be trained to increase the contrast of images, by adjusting the levels of brightness and darkness in the image.
- Colour enhancement: AI models can be trained to adjust the color balance and saturation of images, to make them appear more natural and pleasing to the eye.
- Super resolution: AI models can be trained to increase the resolution of images, by adding more pixels and making them appear sharper and more detailed.

The process typically involves training an AI model on a large dataset of images, using techniques such as deep learning and convolutional neural networks. Once the model is trained, it can be used to enhance new images by analyzing their content and applying the appropriate adjustments.

It is important to note that the quality of the final image enhancement is highly dependent on the quality of the training dataset and the algorithm used. The AI model can also be fine-tuned to specific use cases or type of images to improve the results.

Let talk about some of the use cases

AI can be used to improve images in several ways, such as:

- Image enhancement: AI can be used to enhance the quality of images, by removing noise, improving contrast, and increasing resolution.
- Image super-resolution: AI can be used to improve the resolution of images, by increasing the number of pixels and making them appear sharper and more detailed.
- Image restoration: AI can be used to restore images that are degraded or damaged, by removing artefacts and restoring missing details.
- Image segmentation: AI can be used to segment images into different regions of interest, such as foreground and background, or different objects in the image.
- Object detection and recognition: AI can be used to detect and recognize specific objects within images, such as faces, vehicles, or animals.
- Image generation: AI can be used to generate new images, such as creating realistic images from sketches or generating images from text descriptions.
- Image style transfer: AI can be used to apply the style of one image to another image, such as transferring the style of a painting to a photograph.

- Image compression: AI can be used to compress images, by removing unnecessary information and reducing file size.
- Image annotation: AI can be used to automatically annotate images with labels, captions, or other information, which can be useful for image search and retrieval.
- Augmented Reality: AI can be used to improve images by adding virtual elements to real-world scenes, such as virtual objects, text, or animations.

Introduction to AI and Podcasting

AI in podcasting refers to the use of artificial intelligence (AI) technology to improve and automate various podcasting processes. AI can be used in a variety of ways in podcasting, such as:

- Speech recognition: AI can be used to transcribe spoken words in podcasts into written text, making it more accessible to people with hearing impairments or to people who prefer to read the transcript.
- Natural Language Processing: AI can be used to analyze the transcript and extract useful information such as keywords, topics, sentiment, and entities that can be used to improve the podcast's SEO and increase its discoverability.
- Personalization: AI can be used to recommend podcasts to listeners based on their preferences, listening history, and demographics, helping to increase engagement and retention.

- Podcast summarization: AI can be used to summarize the main points of a podcast episode, making it more accessible for busy listeners or for those who want to catch up on the key points.

- Automation: AI can be used to automate various podcasting processes, such as scheduling, publishing, and distribution, allowing podcasters to focus on creating content and engaging with their audience.

- Audio enhancement: AI can be used to improve the audio quality of podcasts, such as reducing background noise, increasing volume, or improving clarity, making the podcast more pleasant to listen to.

- Podcast creation: AI can be used to generate new podcast episodes, such as news summaries or weather forecasts, by analyzing data and natural language text.

The AI algorithms used in podcasting are generally based on machine learning, which allows them to learn from historical data and make predictions or decisions based on that data. These algorithms can be trained on large sets of podcasting data and can be used to identify patterns and trends that humans may not be able to detect. As the field of AI continues to evolve and more data becomes available, the potential applications of AI in podcasting are likely to increase and become more sophisticated.

For other use case of AI used in podcasting, let me explain in more detail:

- Automatic transcription: AI models can be trained to transcribe speech in audio recordings into text. This can make podcasts more accessible to people with hearing impairments, or those who prefer to read rather than listen. It can also make the podcast more searchable and discoverable.

- Automatic captioning: AI can also be used to generate captions for podcasts, which can be displayed on the screen while the podcast is playing. This can make podcasts more accessible to people with hearing impairments, or those who are in noisy environments.
- Automatic translation: AI can be used to automatically translate the audio of a podcast into different languages, making it accessible to a wider audience. This can be useful for podcasts that have a global reach.
- Speech-to-text: AI can be used to convert speech to text, which can be used to make podcasts more searchable and easily discoverable by adding keywords to the transcript.
- Content analysis: AI can be used to analyze the content of podcasts, such as identifying key topics, speaker emotions, and audience demographics. This can be used to improve the targeting and personalization of podcasts, for example, by recommending similar podcasts to listeners based on their preferences.
- Podcast summarization: AI can be used to summarize the key takeaways from a podcast, which can be useful for people who do not have time to listen to the full episode. This can be done by using natural language processing and text summarization techniques.
- Audio segmentation: AI can be used to automatically segment audio recordings into different segments, such as speech, music, and silence. This can be useful for podcast editing and post-production, as well as for music recommendation.
- Voice recognition: AI can be used to identify the speaker in a podcast and provide information such as the speaker's name, background, and other details. This can

be done by using speaker identification techniques, which can be used to personalize the listener's experience.

- Music recommendation: AI can be used to recommend music or songs that match the mood and theme of a podcast. This can be done by analyzing the audio features of the podcast and recommending music that is similar in terms of rhythm, melody, and other characteristics.
- Podcast Discovery: AI can be used to recommend podcasts to users based on their listening history and preferences. This can be done by analyzing the user's listening history, using natural language processing and sentiment analysis techniques to understand their preferences, and recommending similar podcasts.

Overall, AI can be used to enhance the podcasting experience by making it more accessible, personalized, and discoverable, improving the overall user experience and engagement.

Introduction to AI and Productivity

AI can be used to enhance productivity in several ways, such as:

- Automation: AI can be used to automate repetitive and time-consuming tasks, such as data entry, scheduling, and customer service, freeing up employees to focus on more complex and value-adding tasks.
- Predictive analytics: AI can be used to analyze data and make predictions about future trends, such as sales patterns, customer behavior, and supply chain disruptions, which can help organizations make more informed decisions and improve their operations.

- Personalized assistance: AI can be used to provide personalized assistance to employees, such as helping them find relevant information, scheduling meetings, or providing suggestions for how to complete tasks more efficiently.
- Intelligent search: AI can be used to improve the accuracy and speed of search engines, making it easier for employees to find the information they need.
- Intelligent workflow: AI can be used to optimize workflows, by analyzing data and identifying bottlenecks, inefficiencies, and opportunities for improvement.
- Intelligent scheduling: AI can be used to optimize schedules, by analyzing data and identifying the best times for meetings, appointments, and other events.
- Intelligent RPA: AI can be used to automate repetitive tasks, such as data entry, scheduling, and customer service, using Robotic Process Automation (RPA) techniques.
- Chatbots: AI-powered chatbots can help companies improve their customer service by handling routine queries and providing instant support.
- Resource Management: AI can be used to optimize resource allocation, by analyzing data and identifying the most efficient use of resources such as personnel and equipment.
- Intelligent security: AI can be used to improve security, by analyzing data and identifying potential threats, such as hacking attempts, and responding quickly to prevent them.

Overall, AI can improve productivity by automating repetitive tasks, optimizing workflows, and providing personalized assistance to employees, which can lead to more efficient and effective operations.

Limitation and ethical concerns

We must acknowledge the tremendous progress made in the field of AI and the many benefits that it has brought to society. These benefits can include more efficient and accurate decision-making, improved healthcare and education, and enhanced productivity in various industries.

However, as AI continues to become more sophisticated and widespread, it also raises a number of ethical concerns that need to be addressed. These concerns include issues such as bias, privacy, accountability, transparency, and the potential impact on employment and social inequality. It is important to recognize and address these ethical implications to ensure that AI is developed and used in a responsible and beneficial way for society.

Similarly, despite its remarkable capabilities, AI is still limited in several ways, such as narrow intelligence, data dependence, lack of common sense, limited creativity, and explainability. These limitations can impact the accuracy, reliability, and safety of AI systems, and it is important to recognize them and continue to develop AI technologies in a way that addresses them. By recognizing and addressing both the ethical implications and limitations of AI, we can ensure that we are developing and using this technology in a way that benefits society while minimizing the risks and negative impacts.

Furthermore, it is worth noting that many of the ethical concerns and limitations of AI are interconnected. For example, biases in AI systems can lead to discriminatory decisions that can affect people's lives, and the lack of transparency and accountability can make it difficult to identify and correct these biases. Similarly, the dependence of AI on large amounts of data can raise privacy concerns, especially if the data is sensitive or personal.

Moreover, the limitations of AI can also impact its potential for innovation and growth. For example, the lack of creativity in AI systems may limit their ability to generate new ideas or approaches that go beyond what has been learned from the data.

Here are some of the main limitations of AI:

- Complexity and cost: Developing and implementing AI-based systems can be a complex and expensive process, requiring specialized skills and resources.
- Data quality and availability: AI models require large amounts of high-quality training data to be trained and operate effectively. If the data is incomplete, inconsistent, or biased, it can affect the performance and accuracy of the AI model.
- Transparency and interpretability: Some AI models, such as deep learning algorithms, can be difficult to interpret and understand, making it hard for humans to trust and explain the adjustments made by the AI system.
- Lack of human creativity: AI systems can make adjustments based on the algorithm and data it was trained on, it may not be able to take into account the artistic or creative aspects that a human would consider when adjusting a process.
- Limited applicability: AI-based systems may not be able to process certain types of tasks, such as those that require human creativity, emotional intelligence, or common sense.

- Limited personalization: AI-based systems may not be able to fully personalize the productivity enhancement for each employee, as they rely on general algorithms and data patterns.
- Limited understanding of context: AI-based systems may not be able to fully understand the context of a task, such as the priorities and goals of the organization or the team.
- Dependence on the quality of the algorithm: The performance of AI systems is highly dependent on the quality of the algorithm and the training data used. Poorly designed algorithms can lead to poor performance and inaccurate results.
- Limited understanding of human behavior: AI-based systems may not be able to fully understand and analyze human behavior, which can be important for certain applications such as employee performance evaluation.
- Limited ability to understand the meaning of words: AI-based systems may not be able to understand the meaning of words in a task, which can be important for certain applications such as language translation.
- Job displacement: Automation of certain tasks with AI can lead to displacement of human workers, which can have negative impacts on employment and the economy.
- Privacy and security concerns: AI-based systems that process personal information need to be secure and protect privacy, failure to do so may lead to data breaches and other security issues.
- Ethical concerns: AI-based systems can make decisions that may have ethical implications, and it is important to consider these implications before implementing AI solutions.

- Lack of regulation: There is currently a lack of regulation for AI-based systems, which can lead to issues such as bias and discrimination.
- Limited scalability: AI-based systems may have limited scalability, which can be an issue for organizations that need to process large amounts of data.
- Limited ability to understand humour: AI-based systems may not be able to understand and analyze humour, which can be important for certain applications such as customer service.
- Limited ability to identify new tasks: AI-based systems may not be able to identify new and emerging tasks, which can be important for certain applications such as process optimization.
- Limited ability to understand emotions: AI-based systems may not be able to understand and analyze emotions, which can be important for certain applications such as customer service.

- Narrow Intelligence: AI can excel at specific tasks, but it is still far from having the general intelligence of a human being.
- Data Dependence: AI requires large amounts of data to learn and improve, and the quality of the data can significantly impact the accuracy and reliability of AI systems.
- Lack of Common Sense: AI can struggle to make sense of things that humans consider trivial, such as understanding jokes or sarcasm.
- Limited Creativity: AI can be programmed to generate novel ideas or designs, but it lacks the creativity and imagination of human beings.

- Explainability: AI systems can be difficult to explain, which can limit their adoption in critical applications such as healthcare or finance.
- Ethical Concerns: As noted earlier, the use of AI can raise significant ethical concerns, such as bias and discrimination, accountability, and privacy.
- Cost: Developing and deploying AI systems can be expensive, which can limit their adoption in certain contexts.
- Security: As AI systems become more prevalent, they may become a target for cyber-attacks, which can compromise their reliability and safety.

It is important to recognize these limitations and continue to develop AI technologies in a way that addresses them, so that we can realize the full potential of AI while minimizing the risks and negative impacts.

It is also important to recognize that AI is a rapidly evolving technology, and new ethical concerns and limitations may emerge as it continues to develop. Therefore, ongoing research and development in AI should be accompanied by ongoing ethical considerations and evaluation.

Here are some of the key ethical implications of using AI:
- Bias and Discrimination: AI can reflect the biases and prejudices of its developers and the data it has been trained on. This can result in discriminatory decisions and actions.
- Privacy: AI can collect and analyze vast amounts of personal data, which raises concerns about privacy and security.

- Accountability: AI decisions can have a significant impact on people's lives. However, it can be difficult to determine who is responsible for AI's decisions.
- Transparency: The lack of transparency in AI systems can be a significant concern, as it can be difficult to understand how they make decisions.
- Safety and Reliability: AI systems need to be designed and tested to ensure they are safe and reliable. The failure of AI systems can have significant consequences.
- Employment: The increasing use of AI can have significant implications for employment, as it can automate jobs and potentially lead to unemployment.
- Autonomy: As AI systems become more advanced, they may make decisions that go beyond their programming, raising concerns about autonomy and control.
- Social Impact: AI can have significant social implications, such as exacerbating inequality, and it is important to consider these impacts when developing and deploying AI systems.

Overall, it is important to approach AI with a balanced perspective that acknowledges its benefits and potential, while also recognizing its ethical implications and limitations. By doing so, we can ensure that we are developing and using AI in a way that benefits society as a whole while minimizing the risks and negative impacts.

Final words

After reading this book and you associated artificial intelligence with robots, you can see that's not 100% true. It can be robots, software, programs, learning computers that can impact your day to day life, business and job in 1 way or another.

For a more comprehensive analysis, please refer to AI Revolution.

I will suggest you visit and play around FutureTools.io. You can select any artificial intelligence, free or paid, and trial them in your niche.

FutureTools.io is a library or an aggregator of software and applications that use artificial intelligence (AI). It serves as a one-stop-shop for individuals and businesses to discover, learn about, and access a wide range of AI-powered tools and services.

The platform is designed to make it easy for users to find the right AI-powered tools and services for their specific needs, whether they are looking for solutions to automate business processes, to improve customer engagement, or to analyze data and make better decisions.

It is important to note that FutureTools.io is just one example of an AI-focused library or aggregator, and there are many other similar platforms available that also offer a wide range of AI-powered tools and services. Additionally, it is important to keep in mind that AI is still a rapidly evolving field and new tools and services are being developed all the time, so it is important to stay informed and up-to-date on the latest developments in the field.

Printed in Great Britain
by Amazon

22697139R00040